Excel 365 Conditional Formatting

EASY EXCEL 365 ESSENTIALS - BOOK 2

M.L. HUMPHREY

SELECT TITLES BY M.L. HUMPHREY

EXCEL 365 ESSENTIALS
Excel 365 for Beginners
Intermediate Excel 365
102 Useful Excel 365 Functions

EASY EXCEL 365 ESSENTIALS
Formatting
Conditional Formatting
Charts
Pivot Tables
The IF Functions
XLOOKUP Functions

See mlhumphrey.com for Microsoft Word, PowerPoint and Access titles and more

CONTENTS

Introduction

This book is part of the *Easy Excel 365 Essentials* series of titles. These are targeted titles that are excerpted from the main *Excel 365 Essentials* series and are focused on one specific topic.

If you want a more general introduction to Excel, then you should check out the *Excel 365 Essentials* titles instead. In this case, *Intermediate Excel 365* which covers conditional formatting as well as a number of other topics, such as pivot tables and charts.

But if all you want is a book that covers this specific topic, then let's continue with a discussion of how conditional formatting works in Microsoft Excel.

Conditional Formatting

What is conditional formatting and why might you want to use it?

Conditional formatting is a way to take a data set and apply special formatting to certain results. It makes it much easier to see patterns as well as sort and filter your data.

I often will use conditional formatting in conjunction with a two-variable analysis grid. For example, I might build a grid with number of hours worked across the top and hourly pay rate down the side to see which combinations of hours and pay let me reach my income goal.

Let's say you need to make $500 a week. (I know, I wish that were how the world still worked, but just stay with me here.) Here's what I would put together for something like that:

	A	B	C	D	E	F	G	H
1			Hours Per Week					
2			15	20	25	30	35	40
3	Pay Rate	$ 15.00	$ 225.00	$ 300.00	$ 375.00	$ 450.00	$ 525.00	$ 600.00
4		$ 20.00	$ 300.00	$ 400.00	$ 500.00	$ 600.00	$ 700.00	$ 800.00
5		$ 25.00	$ 375.00	$ 500.00	$ 625.00	$ 750.00	$ 875.00	$1,000.00
6		$ 30.00	$ 450.00	$ 600.00	$ 750.00	$ 900.00	$1,050.00	$1,200.00
7								

I've applied conditional formatting to Cells C3 through H6 so that I can quickly see which combinations of hours per week and pay get me to that goal. 35 or 40 hours per week gets me there for all of the pay rates in the table. But if I can only work 20 hours a week, then I need to be paid $25 an hour or more.

Another place I use this is in my budgeting spreadsheet. There I have my bank account balance set with conditional formatting so that if I ever drop below the minimum balance for free checking, I can immediately see that and fix it before I end up paying an unexpected monthly account fee.

And I use this for the table where I list my revenue, ad spend, and profit from writing each month. I have it set so that each of those fields is shaded from light to dark so that I can easily see the months when I earned the most or least, the months when I spent the most or least on ads, and the months when I was most or least profitable.

That lets me spot trends across the months without looking at eight years' worth of numbers. I don't need to get hung up on the difference between $453.22 and $525.21 when I'm trying to look at trends.

I have another place where I don't even show the numbers at all. I have it set up to display colored bars instead. That lets me easily see how seasonal my results are. (Some products, like winter coats, sell better at certain times of year than others, right? The same thing can happen with different types of books.)

It can be useful to understand those patterns in your own business so that you plan accordingly. I always feel really good in January because that's a strong sales month for my books, but then I feel despair in July, which is not. Having conditional formatting to highlight the annual patterns in my sales reminds me that "this too shall pass", both the good months and the bad ones.

For a more traditional business, you could use conditional formatting to flag customer payments that are more than thirty days overdue. Or to highlight your largest sales transactions. Or flag any expense over $X which should have required pre-approval.

The possibilities are endless.

Another really great thing about conditional formatting is that you can combine it with filtering. So you could flag any customer payments that are overdue and then filter thousands of rows of customer data to only show those entries.

Now that you understand what conditional formatting is and how it works, let's walk through the various options you have in Excel.

First things first, to apply conditional formatting, select the cell range you want to use, and then go to the Styles section of the Home tab and click on the arrow for the Conditional Formatting option to show your available choices:

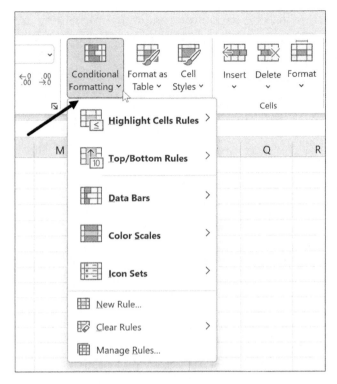

Your other option is to use the Quick Analysis button. To use this, highlight your cell range. You should then see a little icon appear in the bottom right corner of the selected range. Click on that and you'll see the Quick Analysis options.

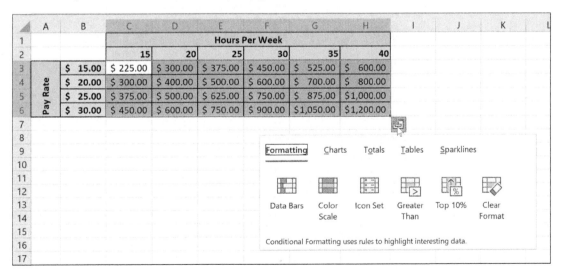

The Formatting tab is the one to use for conditional formatting. Move your mouse over those options and it will show you a preview on your data of what that will look like. The available options are going to depend on the nature of your selected data.

For text entries your options will be Text, Duplicate, Unique, Equal To, and Clear. For entries that contain text and numbers or numbers only, your options will be Data Bars, Colors, Icon Sets, Greater, Top 10%, and Clear.

Quick Analysis comes with its own preset styles that it's going to apply. If you like those styles, then it's a good option. I, at least for the greater than option and the way I use it, always have to change it from the default.

So I'm going to focus from here on out on how to apply conditional formatting using the top menu option, but do know that the quick analysis option exists and may be a quicker choice if you're willing to work with the default settings.

If you ever accidentally end up opening that quick analysis option when you didn't want to (which I have done off and on for years now), use the Esc key to close it. Your cells will remain selected but you won't have to choose one of those options.

Okay. Let's now walk through the conditional formatting dropdown menu from top to bottom.

Highlight Cells Rules

The highlight cells rules are what I used for the example above. What this section does is allows you to apply formatting to cells that meet certain criteria.

Here you can see the set of choices available via the dropdown menu:

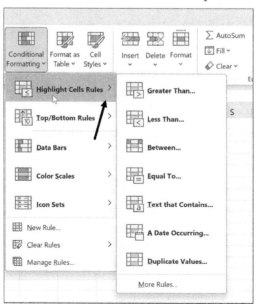

You can choose from Greater Than, Less Than, Between, Equal To, Text That Contains, A Date Occurring, and Duplicate Values. There's also a More Rules option at the bottom that will open the New Formatting Rule dialogue box.

The option I used above was Greater Than (with an edit to make it Greater Than or Equal To), so let's click on that. It brings up the Greater Than dialogue box and immediately colors your selected range of cells based on the default criteria it comes up with and the default format:

	A	B	C	D	E	F	G	H	I	J
1			Hours Per Week							
2			15	20	25	30	35	40		
3		$ 15.00	$ 225.00	$ 300.00	$ 375.00	$ 450.00	$ 525.00	$ 600.00		
4	Pay Rate	$ 20.00	$ 300.00	$ 400.00	$ 500.00	$ 600.00	$ 700.00	$ 800.00		
5		$ 25.00	$ 375.00	$ 500.00	$ 625.00	$ 750.00	$ 875.00	$1,000.00		
6		$ 30.00	$ 450.00	$ 600.00	$ 750.00	$ 900.00	$1,050.00	$1,200.00		
7										

Greater Than ←   ? ✕

Format cells that are GREATER THAN:

$712.50   ↑   with   Light Red Fill with Dark Red Text

> Light Red Fill with Dark Red Text
> Yellow Fill with Dark Yellow Text
> Green Fill with Dark Green Text
> Light Red Fill
> Red Text
> Red Border
> Custom Format...

You can see here it went with greater than $712.50 and the default format is always going to be (or at least has been for decades) Light Red Fill with Dark Red Text.

Not what we want. Click into the box with the value and type in a new value. And then from the dropdown for the format you can either select one of the other options, I used Green Fill with Dark Green text above, or you can go to Custom Format and apply any formatting you want.

For a quick and dirty analysis I would likely type 499.99 into that box, choose the green formatting option, and be done. That's close enough to $500 or more and the fastest way to get my result.

But if it really matters that you have conditional formatting for $500 or more, then the default choices in that dropdown menu under Highlight Cells Rules aren't going to work.

You'll need to use the More Rules option at the bottom of the dropdown menu to have more choices. That, as I mentioned above, opens the New Formatting Rule dialogue box. By opening it through the Highlight Cells Rules dropdown it opens directly onto the "Format Only Cells That Contain" view:

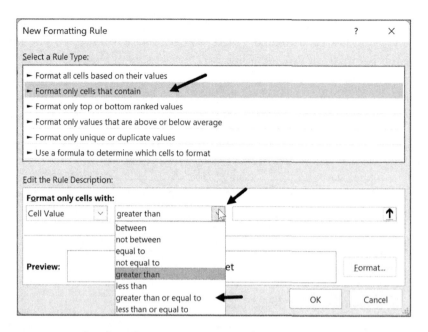

From there you can use the dropdown menu in that dialogue box to choose the "greater than or equal to" option and enter your specific value

But this way of applying a rule doesn't come with preset formatting to choose from like the options available through the Highlight Cells Rules dropdown.

To apply formatting, click on Format to open the Format Cells dialogue box.

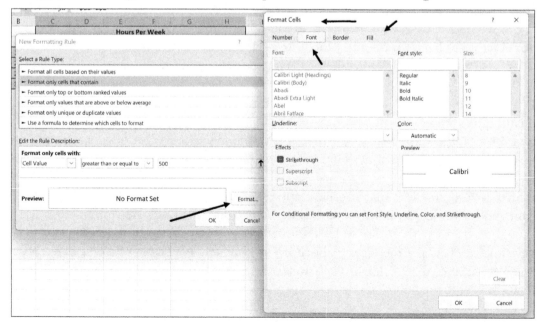

It opens onto the Font tab. That's where you can set the font color and any bolding or underline. But if you want to add a fill like the examples above use, then you'll also need to go to the Fill tab and choose a fill color from there. You cannot edit font or font size but most everything else is available to you.

When you're done click OK.

(Another option if you like Excel's default formats that we'll discuss later is to use one of the default options above, like Greater Than, apply one of the Excel formats, like the green text/green fill one, and then choose to Manage Rules and change the Greater Than option to the Greater Than or Equal To option at that point. That's how I did it. But we're not there yet.)

So. To summarize. Highlight Cells Rules for numbers come with a handful of default choices that you can access through that secondary dropdown menu. If you go that route you also have a handful of pre-defined formats you can apply.

But if you want more options, you need to use the More Rules choice and then you'll have to customize the formatting yourself.

Now let's talk about those bottom three options, Text That Contains, A Date Occurring, and Duplicate Values. I want to start with Duplicate Values because that can still be a numbers one.

Here I've selected Duplicate Values for this range of cells and left it with the red text/red fill formatting:

(Note that you can actually also use this choice to get Unique values by changing the dropdown in the Duplicate Values dialogue box.)

I want to point out one issue to you that makes this one not have a lot of value to me. And that's that it flags all duplicate values with the exact same formatting. So here we have duplicates of $300, $375, $450, $500, $600, and $750. But as far as the formatting is concerned, they're all treated the same.

Which if you did not want any duplicates at all in your data would probably be fine. As long as any cell is formatted with red, you know you still have duplicates.

But what if I wanted to look at my duplicates and figure out which one to keep? This is not a good data set for that, but let's say I had two entries for Students A, B, C, and D in a data table. This conditional formatting option will tell me I have duplicate entries for each of those students, but it doesn't let me easily isolate Student A's duplicate entries. Maybe Student A has three. How do I know that without doing more work? (I'd have to filter by Student A, I couldn't filter by format. And in a table like the one above, that's not an option, so I'd have to use Find to see how many entries I had for Student A.)

Okay. That's the duplicate value option, it may have some limited uses, just keep in mind its limitations.

What about the Text That Contains option? That one works fine, no big surprises.

I used it in the example below to flag all transactions in the Australian Amazon store in this report and it did just fine with it:

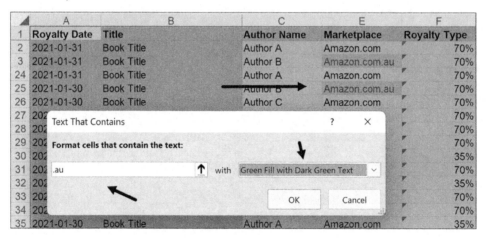

Note here that I'm still in that dialogue box but Excel is showing me what it will do to my data if I click OK. So if you put in criteria and realize that doing so flags entries you don't want to include, you can change it before you click OK. (Or Cancel.)

For example, if I had used "au" instead of ".au" that could have potentially captured other entries I didn't want.

Finally, let's look at the date one:

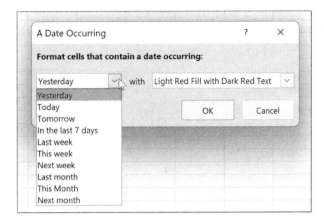

The choices are yesterday, today, tomorrow, last seven days, last week, this week, next week, last month, this month, and next month. I personally don't find this tremendously useful because I can't specify dates or criteria.

If you need one of those, great. But if you need some other set of dates to be flagged, conditional formatting using the Highlight Cells Rules option does not at this point in time give you that level of control. So, for example, "more than 30 days ago" is not an option. Nor is "between this date and that".

Also, the More Rules option doesn't give any additional choices. (This is a place they could make some useful improvements, hint, hint, so maybe that will change over time.)

Okay, next we have the Top/Bottom Rules.

Top/Bottom Rules

Here are the available quick options for that one:

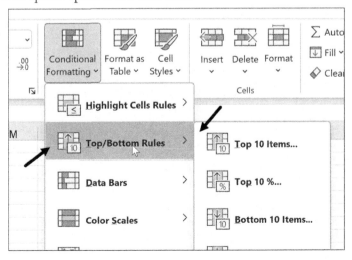

They are labeled Top 10 Items, Top 10%, Bottom 10 Items, Bottom 10%, Above Average, and Below Average. But, when you click on the ten items or ten percent options, you can edit the number in the dialogue box like I have here for the top ten percent option, which I changed to the top twenty percent:

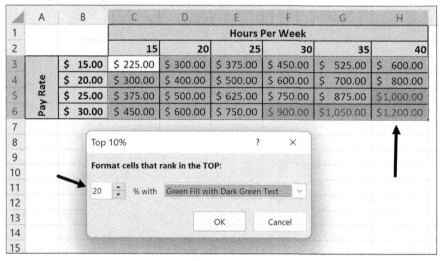

As for formatting, you have the same dropdown menu options as for the Highlight Cells Rules, including the Custom Format option at the bottom of the list.

There is also a More Rules option in the Top/Bottom Rules secondary dropdown menu which will open the New Formatting Rule dialogue box to the "Format only top or bottom ranked values" option, but it doesn't provide any additional options that aren't already listed.

Data Bars

Data bars is the one I mentioned above that I use in lieu of numbers so that I can see seasonal trends in my revenue, ad spend, and profit numbers. What this option does by default is it places a bar in each cell where the size of the bar in the cell is based upon the relative value of the amount in that cell compared to the other cells in the range.

That sounds horribly complicated, but it's not. Let's look at a few examples:

	A	B	C
1	**Example 1**	**Example 2**	**Example 3**
2	1	10	1
3	2	20	100
4	3	30	1000
5	4	40	2500
6	5	50	10000

Here I have three different columns of data. I have applied data bars to each column individually. (That's important, because that means that Column A's values are only being compared to the other values in Column A. Same for Columns B and C.)

Note the values in Column A are 1, 2, 3, 4, and 5. And that the values in Column B are 10, 20, 30, 40, and 50.

The relative relationships between the five values in each of those columns are identical even though the numbers themselves are different. Five is five times one, fifty is five times ten. Same relative relationship. And that's true for all five numbers.

Which is why the data bars you see in those cells are the same. The data bar in Row 2 is one-fifth the size of the data bar in Row 6 for those two columns.

But in Column C the data bars do not work like that, because the numbers I've provided there have a different relationship to one another. 1 is one-ten-thousandth of the final entry 10,000. That's why you can't even see its data bar. 2,500 is one-fourth of 10,000 which is why its data bar takes up one-fourth of its cell.

By default, when working with data bars, the largest value (Y) will have a data bar that takes up the entire cell. Every other value (X) will have a data bar that takes up X/Y portion of its cell. That's why in Columns A and B the data bars are the same size for each row despite the difference in the numeric values, and why each bar is 1/5 bigger than the bar in the row above.

The data bar menu choices are very basic:

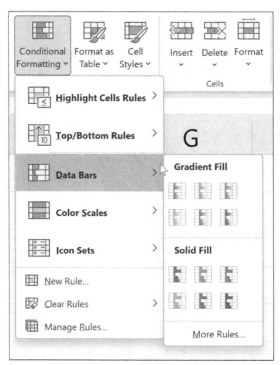

You can basically choose one of six colors in either a solid version (as I did above) or in a gradient version. The gradient shows within each cell. So each data bar shades from darker to lighter, however big that data bar is. Like so:

	A	B	C
1	Example 1	Example 2	Example 3
2	1	10	1
3	2	20	100
4	3	30	1000
5	4	40	2500
6	5	50	10000

Which means that choosing gradient here is just an aesthetic choice. The shading does not give additional information about relative value.

Where things can get interesting with data bars is if you click on that More Rules option and bring up the New Formatting Rule dialogue box. By default, data bars are applied as I described above where it looks at the actual values in the cells and then applies bars based on their relation to one another. But you can change that.

Here, for example, for the data bars in Column B I've set a specific range that is not based on the values in those cells. Now the data bars are applied based upon where a value falls between 0 and 100. That means for each cell the data bar size is determined by the value in that cell (X) divided by 100.

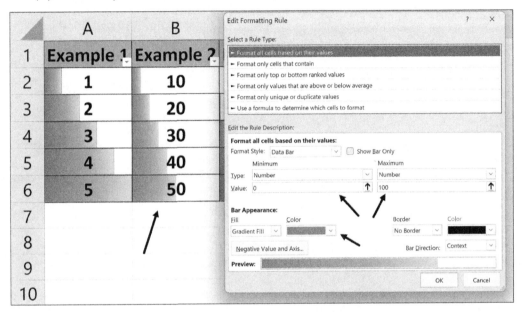

Now 50, our largest value, only generates a data bar that's half the size of the cell.

You can also see that I used the Color dropdown menu to choose a custom color other than one of the six default choices.

The other thing I want to point out to you is that little checkbox for "Show Bar Only". If you don't want to be distracted by the actual values, you can check that box and then you will not see the values in those cells. Like so:

Just be careful on that one. Because, as I showed you at the beginning, data bars for 1, 2, 3, 4, and 5 are going to look identical to the data bars for 10, 20, 30, 40, and 50. So you lose that type of nuance when you hide the values behind the data bars.

Say, for example, these two columns represented sales performance for two sales reps. You'd think that Sales Rep A and Sales Rep B are performing the same, and in terms of percent increase per month they are, but you'd miss the fact that Rep B sells ten times as much as Rep A every month.

Okay. On to Color Scales.

Color Scales

Color scales is one I use a lot. It's the one I use to shade my revenue, ad spend, and profit and loss values per month.

What they do is color a cell a shade of a color or along a continuum of colors based upon the relative value in that cell compared to the values in the rest of the selected cells.

So, much like data bars except color-based. And, like data bars, the secondary menu for this one is color choices:

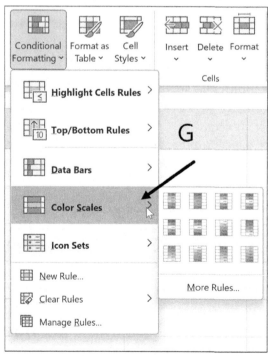

In this case you can choose green-yellow-red, red-yellow-green, green-white-red, red-white-green, blue-white-red, red-white-blue, white-red, red-white, green-white, white-green, green-yellow, and yellow-green.

I almost always use the More Rules option to choose a different color since red, green, and yellow tend to have set meanings of "bad", "good", and "okay". So I'll often use the color dropdown menu and change it so that my color for the lowest value is the lightest color in one of the provided color columns and the color for my highest value is one of the darkest colors in that same column. Like so:

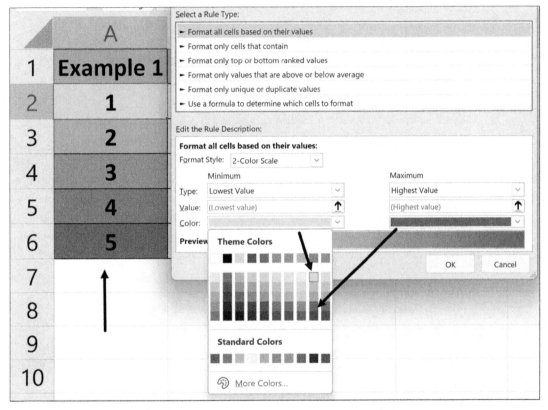

Be careful on this one what colors you choose and what that implies. For example, if I go from gray to orange to brown, which of those colors is "good"? Which is "bad"?

If all you want is to distinguish values from one another, that's fine. But if you're trying to see the "best" results or the "worst" results, take that into consideration when choosing your colors.

Make sure the color you use supports what you're trying to display. At least in the United States, for example, you don't want to shade your "good" values red since red is generally considered "bad". Especially if the other end of the shading spectrum is green which is usually considered "good."

Also, if using a color like red or green, you may want to use multiple colors. Let's say -100 is good and 100 is bad but if it's all shades of red it makes it all look "bad" to one degree or another. Same with all green, it makes it all look "good" to one degree or another.

Two more things to point out here. We've been dealing with set values, but you can also have Excel apply color scales (or data bars) based upon percent, percentile, or a formula that you provide.

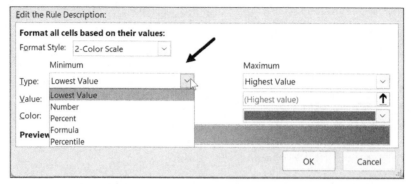

You also have the choice to customize to either a two-color scale or three-color scale by changing the Format Style dropdown.

Finally, if you do have color scales that use a really dark color and you want your values to show in the cell, consider formatting those cells using white text to make the entries more visible.

(You could do this by adding a second conditional formatting rule to that cell range that applies white text to cells with values in that upper range using a custom format and the Highlight Cells Rules. Or if the data is relatively stable, just format those cells with white text manually.)

Okay, next up, Icon Sets.

Icon Sets

Icon sets are much like color scales or data bars, except they show various icons next to the values. Here's the dropdown menu:

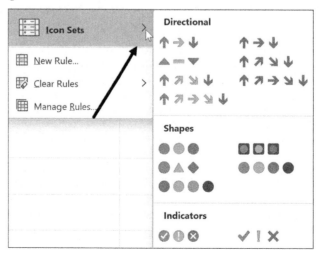

Here are some examples of those in action:

	A	B	C
1	**Example 1**	**Example 2**	**Example 3**
2	↓ 1	● 10	▂ 1
3	↓ 2	● 20	▃ 100
4	→ 3	○ 30	▄ 1000
5	↑ 4	● 40	▅ 2500
6	↑ 5	● 50	▆ 10000

As you can see there are choices that break your data into thirds, fourths, or even fifths, some of which also use color-coding. If you use these icons on your data, Excel will let you then filter your results by icon using the Filter By Color option:

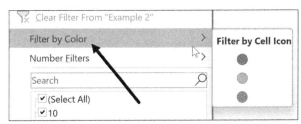

(This is also available if you're using color scales, but not for data bars.)

You can use the More Rules option to bring up the New Formatting Rule dialogue box and customize your icon sets. You can either use one of the same icon sets already shown or combine different elements of an icon set using the dropdown menu:

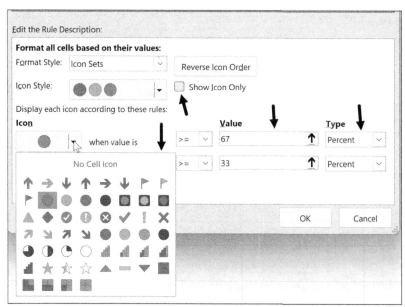

And you can set parameters as percent of the range, number, percentile, or as a formula. Here I've combined icons from three different icon sets and used absolute number values to apply the icons:

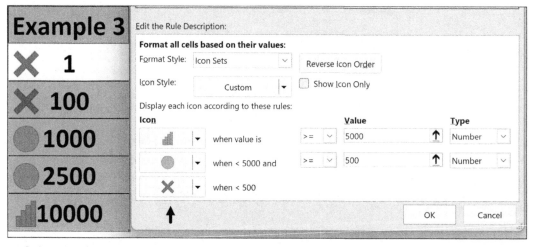

(Proof that just because you can do something doesn't mean you should.)

New Rule

If you just want to jump straight in to customizing a rule and don't want Excel to start you off with any sort of help, you can choose New Rule from the Conditional Formatting dropdown menu in the Styles section of the Home tab.

This will open the New Formatting Rule dialogue box set to the top option, "Format all cells based on their values" and then you can navigate from there.

In general, I wouldn't recommend this. Because as you've seen with the More Rules option on each of the secondary dropdown menus, going to one of those first starts you off on the right screen when you open the New Formatting Rule dialogue box.

In my opinion it's better to know the type of conditional formatting you want to apply and click on the More Rules option from that secondary dropdown menu instead.

The only exception to this might be the final option there, "Use a formula to determine which cells to format". Because if you're applying basic formatting to your cells using a formula (and not applying data bars, color scales, or icons), that may only be possible through this option and there's no quick shortcut to get there.

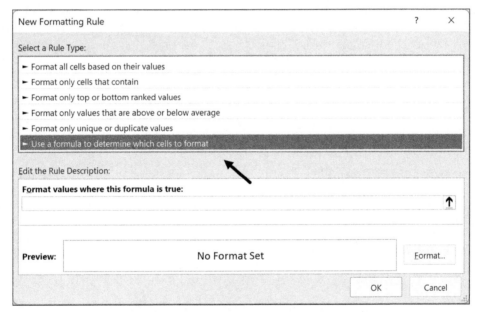

Using Formulas

Okay, so let's talk about using a formula. First, know that the help screen for conditional formatting has a very useful video on this if you want to reinforce what I say here or see another example.

To write a formula for conditional formatting, the formula must return a true or false value and start with an equals sign (which indicates that it's a formula).

For example, let's say that I want to flag those results in Column C where the value in Column B is greater. What you do is write your formula so that it returns a TRUE or FALSE value based upon the first cell in your selected range.

Here, for example, my selected cell range begins with Cell C2:

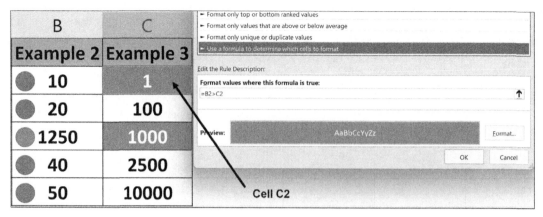

Cell C2

Which means the formula I write in the formula field in my New Formatting Rule dialogue box has to be written for that cell. (I've selected Cells C2 through C6 to apply the formatting, but the cell I write the formula for is Cell C2.)

The formula I wrote is

$$=B2>C2$$

That says, this is a formula (=), look at B2, is it greater than C2? If so, return a value of TRUE, which means format the cell. If not, return a value of FALSE and don't format the cell.

I had it apply a bright green fill and white text. But note that you can also use formulas for data bars, color scales, and icon sets.

The key with formulas is to write them so that they return a TRUE or FALSE result and to write them as if writing a formula for the top cell in the selected range.

Also, you can't reference values in an external workbook although you can reference a value in another worksheet.

Copy Conditional Formatting To New Data

There are a few more topics to cover, but before I forget this and because it's especially useful with dealing with formulas and conditional formatting, if you want to copy conditional formatting from one cell to another, you can use the Format Painter in the Clipboard section of the Home tab.

I just did this a moment ago and it worked like a charm, so hopefully the same is true for you. Click on the cell with the conditional formatting you want to copy, then click on the Format Painter image in the Clipboard, and then click on the cell(s) where you want to transfer that conditional formatting.

I was able to take the formula-based formatting we just created and copy that to Cell F8 with no issues using this approach.

Edit Rules

I will admit that I have been cheating a bit with some of the screenshots you've seen in this section. Because I couldn't show you the conditional formatting applied and the settings I'd applied at the same time using the New Formatting Rule dialogue box. I had to apply the formatting and then go edit the rule to get the dialogue box settings visible next to the formatted cells.

So how do you edit an existing conditional formatting rule? Go to the Conditional Formatting dropdown menu and choose Manage Rules from the bottom of the dropdown menu.

That will open the Conditional Formatting Rules Manager which will default to showing the rules applied to your current selection:

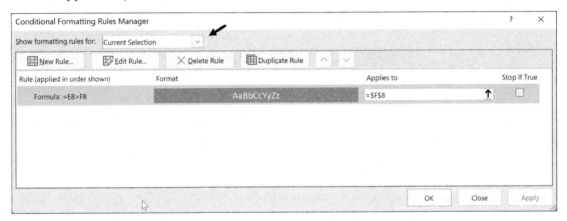

You can change that dropdown to the current worksheet or to any other worksheet in your workbook.

To edit an existing rule, click on the row for that rule and then click on Edit Rule. This will bring up the familiar-by-now dialogue box, but the top of the dialogue box will say that it's the Edit Formatting Rule dialogue box.

Make the changes you want to make and then click on OK. This will take you back to the Conditional Formatting Rules Manager dialogue box where you can either click OK or Apply to make your change. OK will close the dialogue box. Apply will apply the change but keep the dialogue box open.

I will sometimes edit my conditional formatting rules to extend the cell reference range by clicking into the box that lists the referenced cells and editing it. It's probably not the best method to use. But if you do it, do not use the arrow keys while in that box. It will start editing your cell reference range. You need to either click directly where you want to make your edit or backspace to delete the text until you get to that spot.

You can also use the arrow with a bar under it at the end of the listed cell range to select your cell range directly in the worksheet.

I used to have to do this because I would add more entries at the bottom of an existing set of data and the conditional formatting would not carry through to the new entries, but when I was writing this chapter it looks like maybe Excel now extends formatting automatically for you.

Delete Rule or Clear Formatting

If you want to delete a single conditional formatting rule, you can do so through the Manage Rules option in the Conditional Formatting dropdown menu. Click on Manage Rules, find the rule you want to delete, select it, and then click Delete Rule.

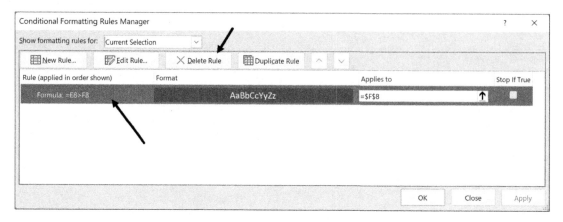

If you want to clear all conditional formatting from a cell or range of cells, though, I think that Quick Analysis option we discussed at the start is faster. Select your cell(s), click on the Quick Analysis icon in the bottom right corner, and then click on the Clear Format option.

There is also a menu option to clear rules from cells. Go to the Conditional Formatting dropdown menu, go down to Clear Rules, and then choose either Clear Rules from Selected Cells or Clear Rules from Entire Worksheet.

(We're going to cover conditional formatting of pivot tables in the pivot table section, but there's an option for that there as well.)

Find Conditional Formatting

If you use the Manage Rules option and choose to look at the current worksheet, that's going to show you all of the rules in that worksheet and which cells they apply to.

But according to Excel, you can also use the Find option to find conditional formatting.

Go to the Editing section of the Home tab, click on the dropdown arrow for Find & Select, and then choose Conditional Formatting from there:

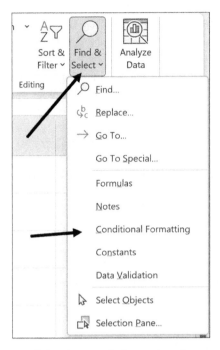

What that does is selects every cell in the worksheet that has conditional formatting applied. They're shaded gray and if you choose to remove conditional formatting from selected cells it will remove it from all of the cells in that worksheet that have conditional formatting applied.

If you want to just find a specific type of conditional formatting, click on a cell that has that type of formatting applied, and then go to the Find & Select option and choose Go To Special. In the dialogue box that appears, click on Conditional Formats, and then choose Same under Data Validation. That will highlight all of the cells that have that specific conditional formatting.

I did have one situation where it did not work where I had used the Format Painter to transfer a formula-based conditional format to a cell that was not in the same column, but otherwise I was able to get it to work.

Multiple Rules

One final thought. It is possible, as I alluded to before when talking about formatting cells with white text if the fill color on that cell is dark, to apply more than one type of conditional formatting to the same cell or range of cells.

Be careful if you do this that the formatting doesn't conflict, because one format may overwrite the other.

There is a "Stop if True" checkbox you can click for a rule to make sure that if there are multiple rules that if one is met no more conditional formatting is applied.

Also, you can change the order of the rules, by using the Manage Rules option to see all rules and then moving a rule above or below the others to get them to apply in the "correct" order. I find that I sometimes just have to experiment a bit to get the result I want.

And since I haven't said it yet in this book, remember that Ctrl + Z, Undo, is your friend. If you do something that looks bad, undo it, and try again.

Appendix A: Basic Terminology

These terms are defined in detail in *Excel 365 for Beginners*. This is just a quick overview in case it's needed.

Workbook

A workbook is what Excel likes to call an Excel file.

Worksheet

Excel defines a worksheet as the primary document you use in Excel to store and work with your data. A worksheet is organized into Columns and Rows that form Cells. A workbook can contain multiple worksheets.

Columns

Excel uses columns and rows to display information. Columns run across the top of the worksheet and, unless you've done something funky with your settings, are identified using letters of the alphabet.

The first column in a worksheet will always be Column A. And the number of columns in your worksheet will remain the same, regardless of how many columns you delete, add, or move around. Think of columns as location information that is actually separate from the data in the worksheet.

Rows

Rows run down the side of each worksheet and are numbered starting at 1 and up to a very high number. Row numbers are also locational information. The first row will always be numbered 1, the second row will always be numbered 2, and so on and so forth. There will also always be a fixed number of rows in each worksheet regardless of how many rows of data you delete, add, or move around.

Cells

Cells are where the row and column data comes together. Cells are identified using the letter for the column and the number for the row that intersect to form that cell. For example, Cell A1 is the cell that is in the first column and first row of the worksheet.

Click

If I tell you to click on something, that means to use your mouse (or trackpad) to move the cursor on the screen over to a specific location and left-click or right-click on the option. If you left-click, this selects the item. If you right-click, this generally displays a dropdown list of options to choose from. If I don't tell you which to do, left- or right-click, then left-click.

Left-click/Right-click

If you look at your mouse you generally have two flat buttons to press. One is on the left side, one is on the right. If I say left-click that means to press down on the button on the left. If I say right-click that means press down on the button on the right.

Select

If I tell you to "select" cells, that means to highlight them. You can either left-click and drag to select a range of cells or hold down the Ctrl key as you click on individual cells. To select an entire column, click on the letter for the column. To select an entire row, click on the number for the row.

Data

Data is the information you enter into your worksheet.

Data Table

I may also sometimes refer to a data table or table of data. This is just a combination of cells that contain data in them.

Arrow

If I tell you to arrow to somewhere or to arrow right, left, up, or down, this just means use the arrow keys to navigate to a new cell.

Cursor Functions

The cursor is what moves around when you move your mouse or use the trackpad. In Excel the cursor changes its appearance depending on what functions you can perform.

Tab

I am going to talk a lot about Tabs, which are the options you have to choose from at the top of the workspace. The default tab names are File, Home, Insert, Page Layout, Formulas, Data, Review, View, and Help. But there are certain times when additional tabs will appear, for example, when you create a pivot table or a chart.

(This should not be confused with the Tab key which can be used to move across cells.)

Dropdown Menus

A dropdown menu is a listing of available choices that you can see when you right-click in certain places such as the main workspace or on a worksheet name. You will also see them when you click on an arrow next to or below an option in the top menu.

Dialogue Boxes

Dialogue boxes are pop-up boxes that contain additional choices.

Scroll Bars

When you have more information than will show in a screen, dialogue box, or dropdown menu, you will see scroll bars on the right side or bottom that allow you to navigate to see the rest of the information.

Formula Bar

The formula bar is the long white bar at the top of the main workspace directly below the top menu options that lets you see the actual contents of a cell, not just the displayed value.

Cell Notation

Cells are referred to by their column and row position. So Cell A1 is the cell that's the intersection of the first column and first row in the worksheet.

When written in Excel you just use A1, you do not need to include the word cell. A colon (:) can be used to reference a range of cells. A comma (,) can be used to separate cell references.

When in doubt about how to define a cell range, click into a cell, type =, and then go and select the cells you want to reference. Excel will describe your selection in the formula bar using cell notation.

Paste Special Values

Paste Special Values is a way of pasting copied values that keeps the calculation results or the cell values but removes any formulas or formatting.

Task Pane

On occasion Excel will open a task pane, which is different from a dialogue box because it is part of the workspace. These will normally appear on the right-hand side in Excel for tasks such as working with pivot tables or charts or using the built-in Help function. (They often appear on the left-hand side in Word.)

They can be closed by clicking on the X in the top right corner.

About the Author

M.L. Humphrey is a former stockbroker with a degree in Economics from Stanford and an MBA from Wharton who has spent close to twenty years as a regulator and consultant in the financial services industry.

You can reach M.L. at mlhumphreywriter@gmail.com or at mlhumphrey.com.

* * *

If you want to learn more about Microsoft Excel, check out *Excel Tips and Tricks* or one of the main Excel 365 Essentials titles, *Excel 365 for Beginners*, *Intermediate Excel 365*, or *102 Useful Excel 365 Functions*.

Printed in Great Britain
by Amazon

46015306R00024